# hello HAPPINESS

## AN ADULT COLORING BOOK
## TO LIVE YOUR HAPPILY EVER AFTER

### KIM GEISER

NORTH LIGHT BOOKS

# CONTENTS

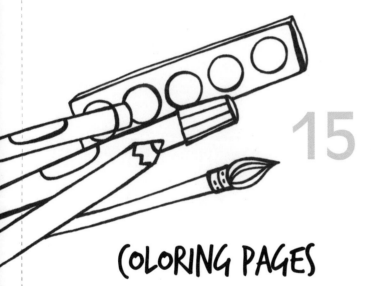

# FINDING YOUR HAPPY PLACE

My entire life, even when times have been tough, I've lived with a big smile on my face. I am a happy person by nature, I suppose, and maybe I'm just lucky that way. But some days are hard; the smiles don't come as easily. On those days, I turn to art! Getting lost in creating something that never existed before is healing and reminds me to return to the place that is my truth—happiness!

I encourage you to use these images as a starting point for making art that showcases your unique style or maybe allows you to find your style. If blank pages intimidate you, think of this as your icebreaker to creativity. Of course, you can just color these pages to relax and unwind, but if you want to take it to the next level, in this first section of the book I share many fun techniques that will elevate the pages to frameable works of art.

I think you will find if you lose track of time coloring these positive pages, you will have a bigger smile to share with the world!

When you finish the pages, fill your space with them as reminders of happiness or read through the ideas provided near the end of the book on how to share them with others.

We can change our own little world with simple kindness and sharing! Start your own happiness revolution!

# HOW TO COLOR HAPPY

In this starting section, I want you to get excited about the coloring materials available to you to use for these happiness-inducing techniques. I will share my favorite brands, but please understand that it's not necessary to go out and buy the most expensive supplies. Quality supplies can offer a happier bang for your buck, but inexpensive supplies work just fine for beginning your journey!

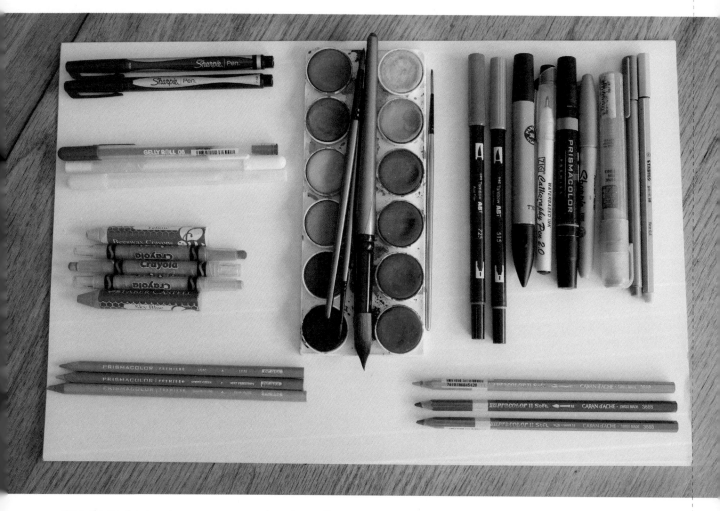

Fine-tip markers, gel pens, crayons, colored pencils, watercolor pans and brushes, assorted markers and watercolor pencils.

# Colored Pencils

I usually say that there is room for all levels of quality with art supplies, but when it comes to colored pencils, I personally don't budge. Prismacolor Premiere pencils are hands-down my favorite colored pencil, and now they offer a Scholar grade pencil. (They are pretty affordable as well!) Their smooth, buttery feel and blendability make them the perfect pencil. I love using them alone, as shown here, or with other mediums, which I will show you in the mixed-media process. Of course, these techniques can be used with any colored pencils, so don't be intimidated.

Using these techniques in different areas of the page, creating a lot of depth and texture, allows you to take the colored pencil to the next level!

Extra tip: Prismacolors actually work very well on a dry acrylic paint surface. The tooth of the paint really grabs the color and makes it POP!

**1** Start with a light layer of color. No need to worry too much about lines or overlapping; it will all blend in later. Use different shades of color to add dimension and interest.

**2** To blend an area, use a white pencil or the lighter color you used as a base. Using a heavier hand, go over the entire area that you colored, making sure to blend out any noticeable marks. This not only blends the colors together, but it also creates a very smooth surface on the paper that you can add even more depth and shadow to.

**3** If you prefer a bold look, using Prismacolors with a heavy hand and intense color is always fun, too! You can get the color even more intense by dipping the tip into mineral spirits. This makes the color almost melt onto the page! Be careful not to use too much, though, because the mineral spirits can stain your page.

# Markers

There are many types of markers out there in all different price ranges. I use them all! Like any of the supplies in this book, you don't need to break the bank to get started on a happy art journey. For this demonstration, I am using Tombow dual-tip markers.

If you are using a high-quality marker, you can also have fun with a blending marker—a colorless marker that will lessen the look of strokes and create a smooth transition between colors or even out one color.

Follow these tips and you are well on your way to mastering markers!

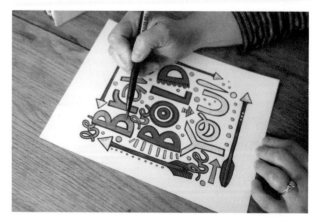

**1** The first layer of color is just a base. Don't worry about overlapping strokes with the base coat. Color the area and let it dry completely. Then pay attention to the base coat and where there are heavy, overlapping strokes and light spots, and fill them in accordingly. When the second base coat dries, you should have a nice even coat of color.

**2** Of course, stopping here with solid coloring is fine, but if you want to take a page to the next level, it's time for shadows and highlights!

Imagine a light source on your page. If the light is coming from the top of the page, the shadows would be cast on the bottom of the images, and a highlight would be on the top where the light would hit them. When beginning to color, keep that in mind, and start with a lighter color for the base coat and go one shade darker to fill in the rest of the area. Using a marker a shade darker than your base coat, you can accent the dark edge of the image with a line along the bottom.

**3** Use a light gray to draw a shadow in the same line directly below the image. This gives the page some depth and makes portions appear to be floating off the page.

## MY FAVORITE MARKERS

- Tombow Markers: Very vivid colors and even coverage
- Sharpie Pens: My drawing pen of choice. Non-bleeding permanent color
- Prismacolor Markers: Vivid colors and easy blending
- Crayola Markers: Inexpensive and washable

# Watercolor

Watercolor is one of those supplies that I use all different brands and qualities. While it's hard to beat fine-quality, expensive watercolor, I find that you can achieve a great look without spending a lot of money. To start out, don't be afraid to borrow the kids' stash! In addition to both transparent and opaque watercolors, I like to use watercolor pencils.

The paper in this book will only take so much water before it is soaked and will tear, but you can use light water on it. For a true watercolor experience, you might want to transfer the image onto watercolor paper or mixed-media paper using graphite paper (see basic instructions in the Mixed Media section).

## OUTSIDE THE LINES

1 To create a completely different look, first wet the entire page and then add lines of color that will blend and mix on the wet paper.

2 Add even more texture to the look by sprinkling salt on the wet paint, allowing it to completely dry, then removing the salt. The salt sucks up the paint and creates a great pitted texture.

3 Now add even more depth with a spatter effect. Simply get the brush full of paint and, using your finger, flick the brush tip toward the paper.

## CONCENTRATED COLOR

1 You can get different results depending on the amount of water you use with watercolor paints. Using just enough water to get the paints wet, you can control the paint and get a lot of detail.

2 To get really precise detail with watercolor, do a loose painting, let it completely dry or blow dry, and then use watercolor pencils as you would colored pencils.

3 Pencil allows you to add shadows and shading in a precise way that is harder to do with a brush. Coming back in with a slightly wet brush, you can then blend the pencil into the background.

# Mixed Media

I covered a few fun techniques on the previous pages, but you might be surprised to find that there's even more joy to be had when you start to experiment and make the pages your own by mixing the techniques together. There are many full-page illustrations in this book, perfect for basic coloring. There are also some that are primarily lettering art or simpler drawings.

These simpler illustrations are great templates for you to explore and create with, adding your own unique spin! My hope is that once you use the techniques I show you, they will give you the confidence to go one step further and use the happy art to really bring out your creativity.

### GEL PENS

I love using opaque gel pens. They allow you to make dark areas pop and to accent light areas. In this piece, I did a watercolor base, then just kept adding texture and detail with the gel pen. Gel pens come in many colors and price ranges, and I use them all. I like that you can really see them pop and that they can be used over most mediums, including watercolor, marker and acrylic. I use them in my coloring pages, on canvases and in my journal. They are great tools to have in your art fun box!

### WATERCOLOR AND COLORED PENCIL

I love using a watercolor base, then accenting the page with colored pencil. The grip that the paint provides on the paper really allows the colored pencil to stick out. Using the techniques from the previous sections, you can use these two mediums together to make a page that is not only frameable, but gift-able, too! Watercolor is great for a background, and colored pencil really brings out the details.

## ADDING DOODLES AND TEXTURE

Just coloring the pages is fun in itself, but why not take it to the next level and really make it *you*. I am a dot girl. I really enjoy using circles to fill a page. Experiment with basic shapes and words, and fill in the empty spaces. The more you play, the more you will discover your favorite shapes and doodles! Since the basic images are done, it's a perfect way to get started on your creative happy art journey!

## JOURNAL PAGES

Many of the pages in this book include words of encouragement that I hope spark thoughts of happiness in you! Using them as journal pages or even just prompts for your own pages is a perfect way to make them your own! Choose a few that speak to you, then remove them and glue them into a journal. If you want to create a book of your own, simply use a hole punch and binder rings, or look up bookmaking tutorials online and really take the pages to the next level!

## ACRYLIC ON CANVAS

Using the transfer technique that follows, any of the images in this book can be made into a beautiful work of canvas art! Simply base coat the canvas in a color of your choice and transfer the image. Once you have the image on the canvas, you can trace over the lines with a black permanent marker such as a Sharpie. Paint in the image with acrylic paints or paint markers, touch up the black lines, accent with a white gel pen and add a little flair of your own. It is an easy way to overcome the fear of a blank white canvas and start thinking about creating your own original art!

## TRANSFERRING IMAGES

Transferring the images onto different substrates is really simple. My favorite transferring technique is using graphite paper. Make a copy of the image by scanning or bringing it to a copy shop. Tape a piece of graphite paper, graphite side down, on a surface such as a canvas, wood or fabric. Then tape the image over the graphite paper, and using a colored pencil and a heavy hand, trace the image. I use a colored pencil so I know what I have and haven't traced. Lift the paper off, and the image is transferred. I like this method because it is easy, inexpensive and can be used for nearly any surface. Of course, there are a lot of image transfer techniques, and I encourage you to use any of them to create projects with these happiness-inducing images.

If you don't have graphite paper, just photocopy the image, cover the back side of the copy with black chalk, place the image side up on the surface and trace. This technique would work best on hard surfaces because excess chalk may get on soft surfaces and muddle the image.

## EMBROIDERY

Using graphite paper, transfer an image onto fabric and use it as an embroidery pattern! What a great way to spread happiness by wearing a creation featuring an uplifting image that you created!

18

COMPLIMENT STRIPS! CUT, COLOR, AND SPREAD SOME HAPPINESS! °%

hello... YOU'RE FUN

hello, SiLLY

I ♡ YOUR, STYLE

YOU'RE So COOL

HiGH Five

That Smile!

Congratulations
ON YOUR AWESOMENESS!

YOU DAZZLE

you SHINE

hello, SUNSHINE

Let's be Friends

YOU INSPIRE me

Get a good Night's Sleep
Wake up Grateful
Eat Breakfast
Move Your Body
Laugh with Friends
Be Kind be Brave
Try Your best
Respect yourself and Others
Go To Bed Happy

82

# Happy Day

# YES! you did it

# YOU are AMAZING

# YOU + Me??? Coffee

# you are so very BRAVE

# IT'S ALL GOOD

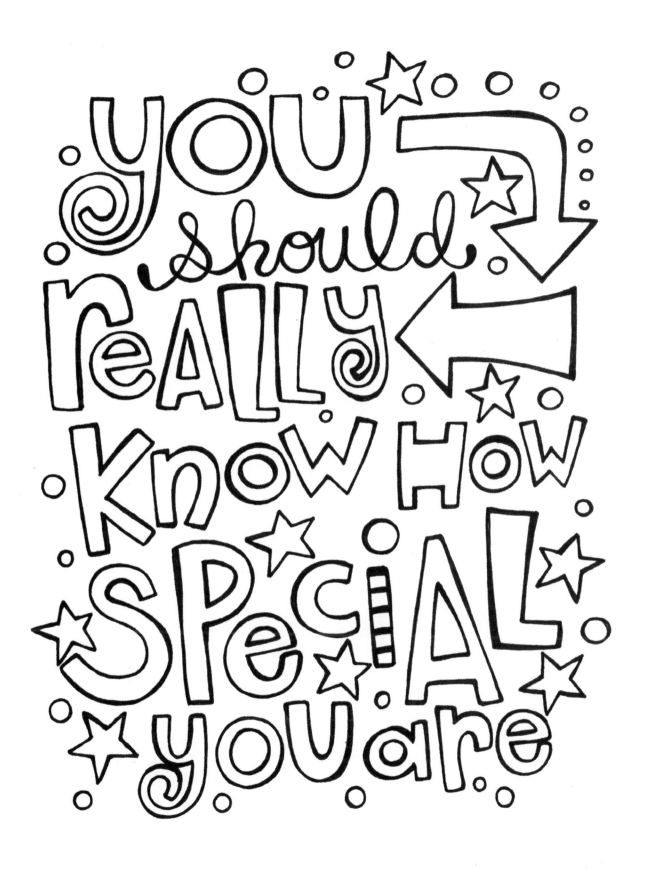

YOU MADE ME SMILE

THANK YOU

I Like YOU

THANK YOU

sunshine Spreader

120

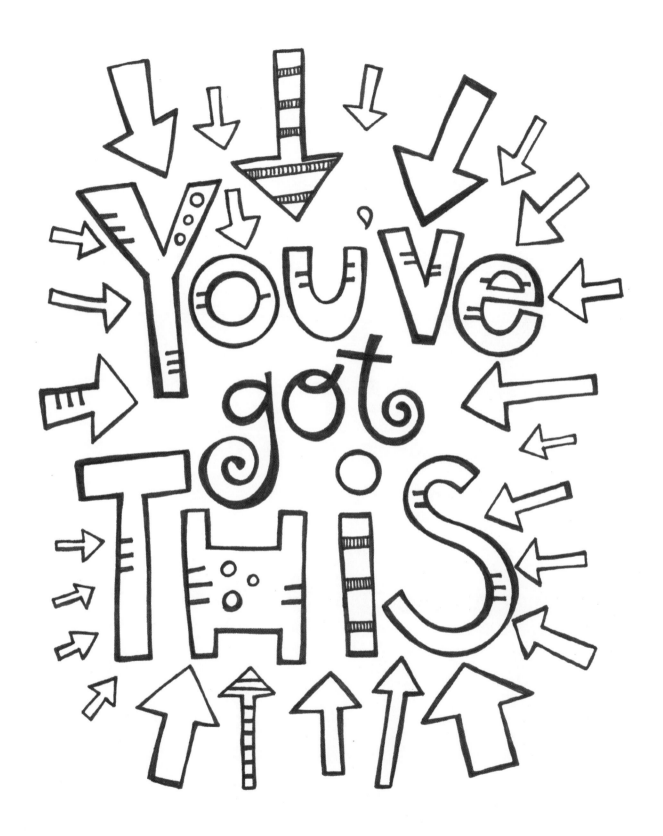

# NOW GET HAPPY!

- Giving is always a perfect key to happiness! So when you are feeling down or want to lift the spirits of someone else, try these little tips. I guarantee you will smile.

- Keep the happy tags in your purse with a pack of crayons. When you go to a restaurant, take them out and color while you wait, then include your finished tag with your tip for the waitstaff!

- Plan a coloring party! Invite your friends over for a fun night of coloring, laughs, good food and drink. Use the techniques in the book to take it a bit further and host a craft night using these happy pictures as a template!

- Fill your home with happiness reminders. Color the pages and hang them around your house on simple clipboards or by using binder clips.

- Give a gift to a friend who is a little down. Embroider the design on a tote bag and fill the bag with comfort gifts like her favorite foods, bath indulgences or anything you know will lift her spirits.

- Spend time coloring with your kids. Take a break from technology and make coloring a fun part of your day. Being creative brings out my happy side every time!

- Give yourself the gift of time alone to do something to feed your own soul. Happiness is a side effect of creativity!

a content + ecommerce company

Other fine North Light Books are available from your favorite bookstore, art supply store or online supplier. Visit our website at fwmedia.com.

21  20  19  18  17   5  4  3  2  1

DISTRIBUTED IN CANADA BY FRASER DIRECT
100 Armstrong Avenue
Georgetown, ON, Canada L7G 5S4
Tel: (905) 877-4411

DISTRIBUTED IN THE U.K. AND EUROPE
BY F&W MEDIA INTERNATIONAL LTD
Pynes Hill Court, Pynes Hill, Rydon Lane, Exeter, EX2 5AZ, UK
Tel: (+44) 1392 797680
Email: enquiries@fwmedia.com

ISBN 13: 978-1-4403-4824-2

Edited by Tonia Jenny
Designed by Jamie DeAnne
Production coordinated by Jennifer Bass
Photography by Olivia Brey - OH Photography

## METRIC CONVERSION CHART

| To convert | to | multiply by |
|---|---|---|
| Inches | Centimeters | 2.54 |
| Centimeters | Inches | 0.4 |
| Feet | Centimeters | 30.5 |
| Centimeters | Feet | 0.03 |
| Yards | Meters | 0.9 |
| Meters | Yards | 1.1 |

# GRATITUDE

I would like to thank so many people for always lifting me up: my wacky, colorful friends, my silly family and everyone who supported me and my art throughout the years.

A special thanks to Jaimie, Jill, Geri, Angie, Shelly, Sallianne, Ellen, Kim and Vanessa. You girls have always been there for me, and I love you.

Thanks to Mom, who always listens to me and loves me.

Molly, you inspire me to be a better example for you and the world. I love your silliness.

Glenn, you have *always* supported my dreams and loved me through the craziness, and I will love you forever.

# ABOUT KIM

Kim is a happy gal who lives a dreamy existence in rural Wisconsin. She spends her days living an artful life by means of her garden, the way she dresses, her love of cooking and, of course, art and jewelry making. She began her journey to art at a very young age and made it her career in 1999 when she opened her first retail store with three other creative ladies. From there she began exploring new ideas and techniques, which led to dozens of publications, featured artist exhibitions, a couple of retail stores and even a spot as the Thrifty Crafter on a local TV station. Kim is an authentically happy person and always hopes to inspire others to live a kind, happy life of their own through her words of encouragement and art-kissed creations.

# Ideas. Instruction. Inspiration.

Receive FREE downloadable bonus materials when you sign up for our free newsletter at ClothPaperScissors.com.

Find the latest issues of *Cloth Paper Scissors* on newsstands, or visit shop.clothpaperscissors.com.

These and other fine North Light products are available at your favorite art & craft retailer, bookstore or online supplier. Visit our websites at artistsnetwork.com and artistsnetwork.tv.

Follow Cloth Paper Scissors for the latest news, free wallpapers, free demos and chances to win FREE BOOKS!

# Get your art in print!

Visit ArtistsNetwork.com for up-to-date information on *Incite* and other North Light competitions.